HISTORY REINTERPRETED

THE MYLES STANDISH HOTEL

ORO EDITIONS
Publishers of Architecture, Art, and Design
Gordon Goff: Publisher

www.oroeditions.com
info@oroeditions.com

Published by ORO EDITIONS INC.

TEXT BY
Patrick Ahearn

WRITTEN WITH
Caroline Castellan Stone

COVER IMAGES
Taylor Ahearn

P.A. ARCHITECT MARKETING DIRECTOR
Katherine Nolan

P.A. ARCHITECT MARKETING
Caroline Castellan Stone

ORO EDITIONS MANAGING EDITOR
Jake Anderson

BOOK DESIGNER
Katherine Nolan

Typeset in Rieux and Minion Pro

10 9 8 7 6 5 4 3 2 1 FIRST EDITION

Library of Congress data available upon request.

ISBN: 978-1-957183-14-5

Color Separations and Printing: ORO GROUP LTD.
Printed in China.

International Distribution: www.oroeditions.com/distribution

ORO EDITIONS makes a continuous effort to minimize the overall carbon footprint of its publications. As part of this goal, ORO EDITIONS, in association with Global ReLeaf, arranges to plant trees to replace those used in the manufacturing of the paper produced for its books. Global ReLeaf is an international campaign run by American Forests, one of the world's oldest nonprofit conservation organizations. Global ReLeaf is American Forests' education and action program that helps individuals, organizations, agencies, and corporations improve the local and global environment by planting and caring for trees.

HISTORY REINTERPRETED
THE MYLES STANDISH HOTEL

PATRICK AHEARN

CONTENTS

INTRODUCTION

In my near 50-year architectural career, I've developed a practice focused on timeless homes that are intrinsically linked to the past while living seamlessly for present day. Whether actually historic or historically inspired, my residences balance preservation with modern innovation and are carefully designed to improve the lives of those who experience them, whether as homeowners, visitors, or mere passersby.

OPPOSITE: In this undated early photo, two women stroll along a 400-foot pier toward the hotel, the Duxbury Yacht Club to their right, the Myles Standish Spring to their left.

In my first book, *Timeless*, I explained how I adapted and applied the idea of philosophy's greater good theory to my practice of architecture and highlighted how good design can positively impact the lives of a home's inhabitants and help build a sense of community for the general public. In an exploration of works from preservation and renovation to modernization and new builds with imagined histories, I examined the many ways in which architecture can enhance how we live.

This volume, however, represents something different. On these pages, I'm pleased to share a reinterpretation of the past—a story of reimagination along with an uncanny connection that has offered me the opportunity to hold hands with history while moving toward the future time and again. Allow me to explain.

A project in the first suburb
In 2016 I received a phone call from prospective clients about a commission in Duxbury. Deeply steeped in American history, Duxbury is a coastal community about 45 minutes south of Boston. The town was founded on land that Native People inhabited as early as 20,000 years ago according to archaeological evidence. An area prized by the Wampanoag Nation of people for its natural bounty, Natives harvested fish from the bay and waterways along with corn and game from adjacent shores. In 1617–1618, European pathogens decimated much of the Native population and the healthy fled from the sick, abandoning the area. When Pilgrim colonists in Plymouth looked to move beyond their original settlement in 1627, Duxbury's then uninhabited shores called, arguably making it the first suburb.

"The unequaled quality of the air of Duxbury, always inspiring and invigorating, cooled in summer by the waters of Plymouth Bay and yet not made humid by the stretch of ocean on the side of the prevailing winds; the purity of the water with which the hotel is supplied; the opportunity for rest and yet the variety of amusements with the visitor finds; the book of history ever open, and from which the student may learn lessons concerning the birth and progress of New England life, cannot fail to make this house a favorite resort for those who seek a summer residence near the sea."
—Early hotel advertisement

Architecturally, Duxbury is notable for its textbook examples of well-kept early houses which survive to this day. Classic Yankee pride of ownership is evident at every turn. Capes, saltboxes, Greek Revivals—they're all present and preserved within a quintessential coastal town.

OPPOSITE: Guests arrive at the Myles Standish Hotel in an early automobile near the turn of the century. I sought to revive the feeling of a prominent welcoming porchfront in the renovation.

PATRICK AHEARN

STANDISH HOUSE,

South Duxbury, Mass.
OPENS JUNE 10, 1874.
Chas. C. Knapp, - Proprietor.

Thirty-five miles from Boston on Old Colony Railroad.   One hour and thirty-five minutes' ride by Express train.

This new and beautiful Hotel is located at South Duxbury, Mass., in close proximity to CAPTAIN'S HILL, and other interesting scenes connected with the history of the Pilgrim Fathers.   The facilities for boating and fishing are unsurpassed anywhere.   The temperature of the sea water, here being several degrees higher, renders sea bathing at this place a positive luxury.   The location being near Boston, among the coolest and healthiest on the whole coast, makes the Standish House one of the most desirable Summer Resorts for Boston business men and their families.   Extensive forests of pine and spruce are in close proximity, and over one hundred ponds, lakes and brooks are situated within ten miles and are well supplied with pickerel and trout.   A good stable is connected with the house.

☞ TERMS: Three dollars per day. Ten to fifteen dollars per week
☞ For furthur particulars apply to the proprietor.

TIME TABLE, OLD COLONY R. R.
Leave Boston, 7.40 A. M., 2.30 and 4.45 P. M., also 6.15 P. M., Saturdays.
Return, leave So. Duxbury, (5.00 A. M., Mondays) 6.50, 8.20 A. M., 3.10 P. M.

OPPOSITE LEFT: One of the oldest surviving advertisements for the Myles Standish Hotel (circa 1874) touts the location as one of the most desirable resorts for prominent Bostonians and their families.

OPPOSITE RIGHT, TOP AND BOTTOM: The hotel's owners capitalized on a natural spring on site which the Puritans allegedly used for drinking water a century prior. They tapped the spring, producing beverages lauded for their healing qualities. These labels date to 1900.

ABOVE: Three children play at the Duxbury Bay beach with the Myles Standish Hotel in the background in this 1910 photograph.

FOLLOWING PAGES: This early photograph shows the hotel in its prime, with a porch wrapping the structure on two sides, an intact three-story center with mansard roof, and functional third floor awnings. The cannon did not survive to present day, though a lone cannonball remains.

PATRICK AHEARN

With streets that put forth a living primer on classic vernacular, Duxbury is New England authentic down to the cedar shingles weathered to iconic grey thanks to the Atlantic's salt spray.

Oddly enough, the property I was called about didn't begin as a home at all. A resort built in 1871 and subsequently known as the Myles Standish Hotel, the structure was intended to be a shining anchor within a new development next to land granted to storied Pilgrim Captain Myles Standish in 1627.

In its heyday, the hotel lured well-heeled guests from Boston to New York who made the long trip to Duxbury via rail, boat, and stagecoach. The air on the property was filled with the sounds of weekly balls, patriotic sing-along concerts, and regular regattas. Bells were rung to cue multicourse meals featuring the bay's very own clams along with fresh fish, vegetables, and decadent desserts. At its height, a natural spring once used by the Pilgrims for drinking water was tapped for the resort's very own bottling company, which produced ginger ale and seltzers heralded for their purity and healing properties.

But time was unkind to the Myles Standish Hotel. Fire destroyed hotel outbuildings in 1908, and 1914 marked its final summer season. Two brothers-in-law somewhat reluctantly purchased the defunct resort plus surrounding lots which never quite took off as intended. They chose to raze the center section of the structure to achieve a summer residence out of each wing. In 1946, the south wing was moved off-property.

Fast-forwarding nearly 100 years, neighbors of the hotel's north wing saw potential in the bones of the old building and hoped to save it from being demolished. In addition, they felt some responsibility for preserving history— their abutting home was constructed on land once belonging to the resort, making them ideal shepherds for the half-hotel.

But a resort once glittering and proud was now overgrown with shrubs and weeds. Little-used by its owners in the recent past, the interior layout was convoluted at best, and the exterior presentation was nearly incomprehensible. The structure required significant rehabilitation, reimagination, and reinterpretation. I was glad to be put to task.

Lessons learned from the past
There were many past lessons to call upon as I considered a new program for the Myles Standish. In truth, this wasn't my first dance with a historic hotel. My hand has touched a number of classics over the years, including Boston's Copley Plaza and Washington DC's Shoreham Hotel. But perhaps most relevant to the Myles Standish was my reinterpretation of the Equinox Resort in Manchester, Vermont's historic district. Like the Myles Standish, the Equinox was developed as a resort destination in the late 1800s and had experienced a number of unfortunate renovations over the years. At the Equinox, the goal was to create new spaces that tugged at the sentiments of memory while improving the interior organization, all while elevating the exterior without sabotaging the structure's sense of place.

PREVIOUS PAGES: Two hotel wings appear in this undated photograph, though the mansard-roofed center is missing. Prior to one structure moving off site, the two were adjoined via porte cocheres and a pergola. Modified rooflines and chimneys are also seen.

ABOVE: In the Manchester, Vermont, historic district, renovation and reimagination at the Equinox Resort including the newly developed arrival sequence shown here elevated the resort for modern day while respecting its storied past.

PATRICK AHEARN

The Equinox would maintain its identity as a hotel, and at every turn, design choices were made to recall historic inns of the past. I reconfigured the arrival sequence to introduce a new sense of procession to the entrance, with details like marble sidewalks and a circular drive specifically inserted to serve purposes of practicality and romanticism. The front door was relocated to afford the addition of a more modern two-story space behind the lobby, and a new central spine was added from which a lively bar and fireplaced gathering rooms could be accessed. The spine would resolve at the Marsh Tavern, a new eatery configured out of a vacant meeting room. The tavern was planned and presented as though it could have been there since the hotel's inception, complete with period-appropriate architectural detailing and traditional menu choices.

After the renovation, I distinctly recall sitting in the Marsh Tavern with investors. While lunching on split pea soup, I overheard a nearby diner waxing poetic, "remembering" being in the tavern as a child, an impossibility since the restaurant hadn't existed back then. This was the precise human response I had hoped for as we planned the renovation, and is always my goal

when working with historic properties. Guests of the Myles Standish would have passed away decades prior, but I wanted to elicit a similar feeling of nostalgia from those who would experience the resort as a residence once the renovation was complete.

In thinking about the Myles Standish Hotel, I also drew from lessons learned while reinvigorating Boston's Faneuil Hall marketplace and Quincy Market even earlier in my career. In 1976, as a young architect at Benjamin Thompson and Associates, I created a script for the revitalization of the landmark destination, weaving together a story of past and present. What was once a thriving marketplace and meetinghouse had fallen into significant disrepair, and our team presented a concept that would breathe new life into the locale.

Without the assistance of computer generated drawings or 3D visualization, I hand drew what was and what could be, developing a narrative to demonstrate how a tired landmark could become a vibrant year-round destination. Complete with new indoor-outdoor connections thanks to rising doors which linked storefronts with open corridors, the story became one of a bustling, pedestrian-friendly European-style marketplace. Even the spaces in between buildings were carefully considered with historic cobblestones resolving in spaces for street performers, new streetlights, and outdoor seating for cafés and restaurants. I pursue this narrative-driven approach in my residential work today, and would apply it in the Myles Standish renovation

OPPOSITE: Early in my career, the revitalization of Boston's Faneuil Hall and Quincy Market taught me how narrative-driven architecture could have a meaningful impact on people's lives. I applied those lessons to my reimagination of the Myles Standish Hotel.

PATRICK AHEARN

along with significant attention to indoor-outdoor flow and the space between structures.

I also built upon my experience with hundreds of renovation and preservation projects over the years, in particular those in the historic village of Edgartown on Martha's Vineyard, in my hometown of Wellesley, Massachusetts, and throughout coastal New England. In a sense, the Myles Standish would be the preservation of an *idea*, not necessarily a structure. We wanted to communicate that history had happened on site more than we wanted to preserve the exact half-hotel that remained on the property. The renovation would require operating with care, proceeding with a sensitive eye toward original architectural elements, the spirit and scale of which I intended to keep in the transformation.

Attention to the overall tapestry of details—a hallmark of my renovation work—would be unquestionably applied at the Myles Standish as well. Historically motivated coach lighting astride doorways, white clapboard siding, Essex green shutters and doors, regionally appropriate materials like bluestone, fieldstone, and cedar shingles—all would be on display in the finished product. I sought to backdate the overall residence via careful specifications indicative of a historic composition, making the new home true to the intentions of yore while living logically for its new owners and those in the generations to come.

An uncanny connection
Many New Englanders are proud of their bloodlines which can be traced back to early colonists. Entire organizations like the Sons and Daughters of the American Revolution are devoted to celebrating the roots of citizens whose ancestors helped establish our nation and lived in early suburbs like Duxbury. I wholly respect those groups but don't qualify for membership; my roots are proudly linked to the working class planned suburb of Levittown, New York, which I discuss in great detail in my first book and in my complimentary online course *Patrick Ahearn's Studio.*

While my ancestors may not have rubbed shoulders with Captain Standish or his comrades, it seems he and I have become well acquainted over the years. The Myles Standish project was sited next to land owned by Captain Standish in 1627, and roughly 300 years later, my personal residence was designed for Captain Standish's seventh-great-grandson by celebrated architect Royal Barry Wills. At my own home I renovated, expanded, and reimagined much in the way I would do at the Myles Standish, stepping new additions back from the main structure and using

Scan the code to visit studio.patrickahearn.com.

OPPOSITE: A jovial back porch moment was featured in one of the earliest Myles Standish Hotel brochures. In this renovation, I sought to preserve the idea of the porch as a place to greet and gather.

authentic materials and fixtures to seamlessly re-create a story that Wills himself could have told had he considered a different program. I'm hopeful the Standishes might appreciate what I've done with their properties.

Some leave their mark on history by exploring new shores, their triumphs commemorated with fanfare and monuments. My architectural achievements are most successful when I'm a ghost in the night, when my hand is unnoticeable to even the most trained eye. I'm proud to accept my humble place in history, carefully reinterpreting the past while preserving a sense of place through classically motivated design. I hope the discussion of the project in the pages that follow will inspire others, whether in creating a place of their own or in finding their own place in history. It is an honor to continue to do this work.

OPPOSITE: Guests enjoy views of the bay from comfortable rocking chairs along the back porch in an undated photograph from one of the earliest Myles Standish Hotel brochures.

Chapter 1

CREATING A HISTORICALLY INSPIRED NARRATIVE

For each project I complete, part of my process is developing a distinct narrative for the property. This sort of scripting helps to drive authentic-feeling design choices for each home and to create a convincing finished product, whether the residence is one of historic preservation, renovation, or a new build on vacant land. At the Myles Standish Hotel, part of the joy of the project was flipping the script from one of tragedy to a tale of triumph.

OPPOSITE: A view of the new front entrance to the residence, with an open porch that all but opens its arms to welcome family, friends, and guests.

LEFT: When my clients purchased the residence in 2016, the main entrance faced the back of the property, which wouldn't suit an estate today. Disjointed modifications made over time left the structure lacking in cohesion and architectural clarity.

PATRICK AHEARN

HOTEL BARELY SAVED

Myles Standish in Danger From Fire Which Destroyed Stables

1908

DUXBURY, July 12.—An opportune change of wind was all that saved the exclusive Myles Standish Hotel from complete destruction late tonight, when the stables, garage and outhouses connected with the establishment caught fire.

The fire started in the garage about 30 feet from the hotel. Before it was discovered it had gained such headway that it was impossible to save the cars. Two of them, belonging to Mr. William S. Bache and Mr. E. E. Wood of Boston, were destroyed.

The fire, which gathered great headway, broke out at about 11 o'clock.

Near a Panic

It soon spread from the garage to the stables and the other outhouses, which are very close to the hotel. Most of the guests of the hotel had retired for the night, and they were awakened by finding their rooms filled with smoke. There was nearly a panic in the endeavor to get out of the hotel.

The main building of the hotel was just beginning to catch fire from the sparks when the wind changed and a dozen small fires were extinguished before they had eaten in.

The total loss to the buildings will be about $5000, and the loss of the autos will be about $15,000. The cause is thought to have been spontaneous.

PREVIOUS PAGES: In the center of this undated photograph, the Myles Standish Spring is noted beneath a gazebo. The pier carefully wrapped around the spring, which was surrounded at the bottom by what appears to be regionally sourced fieldstone.

LEFT: A fervent description of the 1908 fire at the Myles Standish Hotel which destroyed two automobiles, the garage, stables, and outhouses on site before causing sparks in the central portion of the hotel. The cause of the fire is still unknown.

I vividly remember visiting the existing house for the first time. I was struck by the underwhelming presence the structure had from the street and the promise and potential that it held within. The owners shared an undated historic photograph, which explained part of the building's unfortunate end. In the picture, two separate wings of the old hotel are seen. The remnants of a covered porch that at one point ran the length of the bay side of the resort are shown on each half-hotel. Porte cocheres, likely built from remnants of the partially destroyed covered porch, are shown on each house. These architectural canopies may have been added in an attempt to make sense of main entrances which faced the back of the property. In the late 1800s when visitors arrived by boat, these entrances made clear sense. From the street today, however, they would give a cold shoulder.

The clients' photograph was most significant for what it was missing—the central portion of the Myles Standish's original structure. In 1908, a fire filled guest rooms with smoke in the late hours of the evening[1]. After the incident, the hotel was never quite the same. When investor brothers-in-law eventually purchased the hotel, they razed the center portion of the resort, and each kept a wing as a residence. This backstory to the clients' photograph helped answer how and why we were left with an illogical structure on site,

and also provided ideas for a brighter new story for the renovation.

My goal as an architect was to write a new script for my clients' house, one that would have been possible had the original hotel been smaller in size and narrower in scope. The job would not be one of exact restoration, because more than half of the original building was missing. I wanted to create a new home using some parts of the existing structure, which would tell a story of a New England seaside inn that was added onto over time and which now lived vibrantly as a residence. Every element—from the pitch of the roof to materials used and window details—everything would be derived from that narrative.

While achieving these goals, an even more critical task was to listen to the homeowners' wants to deliver a renovation that would be all they imagined and more. An established Boston-area family, my clients wanted the property to be a functional long-term home, which meant addressing the prospects of aging in place while having space for grown children and grandchildren to visit and stay. Space for entertaining was important and a substantial program for outdoor living was a definitive ask. They requested a dedicated office space for the husband and an additional office area for the wife, plus a fitness center of some sort on-property. Most important, the homeowners wanted to capitalize on long views of Duxbury Bay from main living areas and bedrooms, especially the primary bedroom suite.

I am of the firm belief that zoning

---

[1] "Hotel Barely Saved: Myles Standish in Danger from Fire Which Destroyed Stables" 1908

PATRICK AHEARN

dictates design. When dealing with a property of this structure's vintage, I regularly have a local historical commission to appease, though each municipality's rules are unique. While the Myles Standish Hotel was located outside of an identified historic district in Duxbury, its age placed it under the purview of the town's historical commission. I would have to study local requirements and present at public hearings to eventually gain the commission's approval. As always, my goal was to capture the history of the place and create a plausible architectural execution that could have been conceived almost 150 years prior. I took great care to create a believable structure that would welcome visitors in a way the Myles Standish Hotel could have done in its prime.

Using my experience at the site visit, the clients' historic photograph, and many subsequent conversations with the homeowners, I began to draw. My firm gladly puts forth digital renderings and floor plans and uses ever-evolving technology to demonstrate our designs. I, however, prefer to begin with pen and ink. The drawings included in this book are representative of my early ideas for the Myles Standish.

To communicate the new narrative, I began at the curb. An impressive existing stone wall delineating the property along the street would be the cue upon which a much more anticipatory sense of arrival was built. I proposed a processional peastone driveway with a cobblestone border which would resolve at a new street-facing front door and motor court and would wrap around an enormous tree in the front yard.

This sort of long winding drive is typically seen on the approach to grand country manor estates of the late 1800s and early 1900s. In addition, newly suggested landscaping would help identify boundaries and provide privacy from abutters.

My proposed renovation was motivated by the design of the original wing, recalling the past and respecting its context. The prominent covered porch formerly seen only at the rear would also be added at the front, providing a friendly greeting for guests at a logical main entrance. Inserting previously lacking symmetry, the front door would sit at the center of the main house flanked by a pair of sidelights with a transom window above. A new carriage house was proposed, which would be linked to the main structure via a connector wing. The resulting ensemble would read as though it had been an inn which triumphantly survived the test of time, with a boathouse that was added at a later date and subsequently attached to the main residence. Architecturally, the new script was written.

This new script, however, would not only benefit the homeowners. A clear example of *architecture for the greater good*, the new narrative would encourage friendly interaction and benefit the community and passersby as well. From the street, the front door would beckon to visitors to stop in, and the one-story stepped-down connector wing would preserve public views of the bay beyond the property.

At the back of the house, a comprehensive program for outdoor living was presented. In addition to the covered porch, an element that

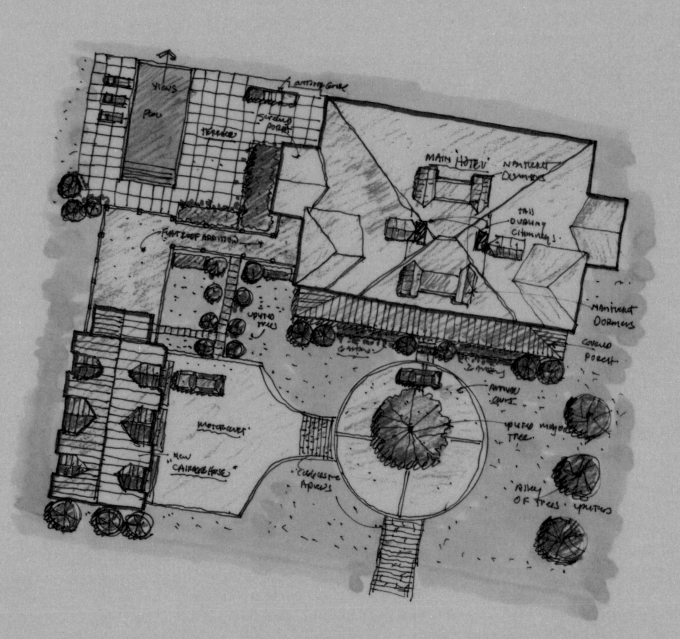

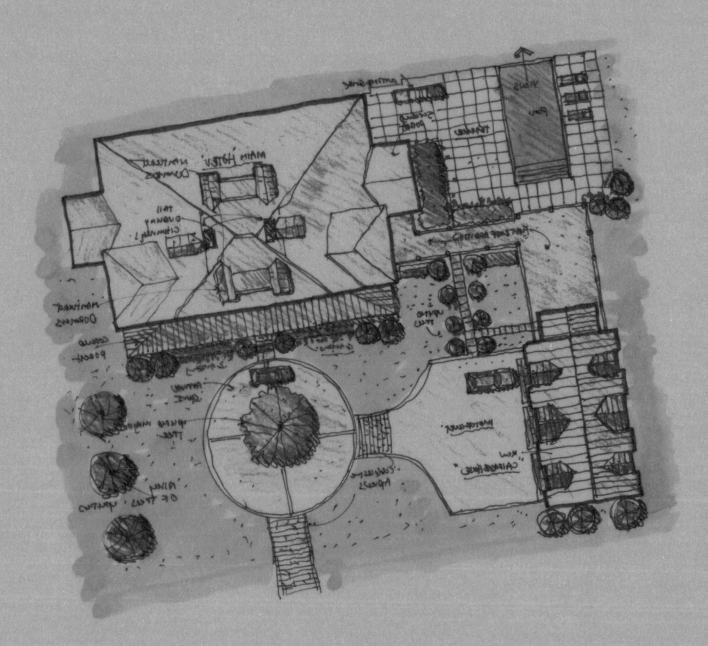

POOL HOUSE   CONNECTOR   COVERED PORCH

ARRIVAL COURT   GRAND ENTRY SEQUENCE

would be rethought and reintroduced in slightly different fashion, the residence would also include a three-season porch and significant hardscape with space for outdoor cooking, dining, conversation, and poolside relaxation. To fully respect zoning laws, all elements were kept out of the 200-foot buffer from the shoreline and a significant rear lawn was maintained.

On the interior, the layout would be completely rethought in order to eliminate the rabbit warren of rooms left over from the home's former life as a half-hotel. A new center spine would run from the foyer through the dining area out to the porch and yard beyond. Seen in much of my work, this central spine helps to organize and anchor the home's floor plan and allows for appreciation of water views from the moment a person enters the home.

Along the back of the house, family living spaces were all strategically placed with walls of windows and French doors, all but bringing the outside indoors. A first floor primary bedroom suite would also overlook the water and satisfy the clients' ask for the ability to age in place. In the proposed connector wing, sets of French doors could be opened simultaneously for a direct path from the motor court to the back patio and pool for easy summer entertaining. The bayside augmentation of the carriage house would function as a pool cabana, housing a shaded and cooled sitting room along with a lavatory. In addition, by considering a second floor within the carriage house, the clients could achieve a surprising and bright home fitness center.

On the residence's second floor, family

bedrooms would be reconfigured for privacy and comfort. Proposed to all be en-suite, the bedrooms would provide separate getaway spaces for the clients' children and grandchildren. Three out of four bedrooms would enjoy water views and two would feature exterior balconies.

Where two somewhat claustrophobic bedrooms were previously housed on the third floor, a new open office space was specified. With captivating views out arched dormer windows, the office met the homeowners' goal of a dedicated workspace away from the bustle of daily activity. While the original third floor was devoid of architectural trim and detail, my plans called for their insertion, elevating the upper level to the same impressive architectural standards of the first and second floors.

After conversation and revision with the clients, the plans for renovation were approved, and a new story for the Myles Standish Hotel was ready to be written.

OPPOSITE: The proposed site plan shows a new anticipatory arrival sequence along with whole-house programming that reads as a complete thought.

FROM THE STREET

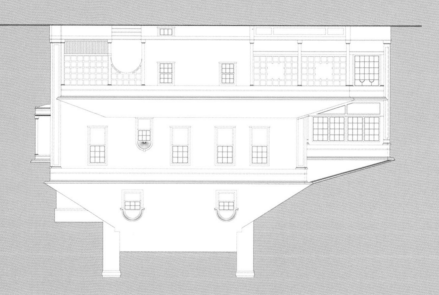

On the existing structure, this was the convoluted façade that greeted visitors. Enclosed sunrooms on the first and second floor together with inconsistent trelliswork along the front presented dizzying patterning and made for an ambiguous entry. The reimagined front façade would introduce balance and symmetry to the main residence along with a definitive front entrance and a carriage house program previously lacking on site. Importantly, the historic narrative would be established from this perspective, even to passersby.

FACING SOUTH

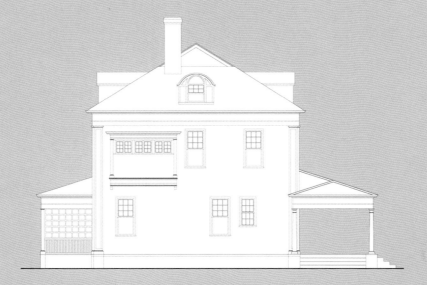

Originally, this side of the structure would have connected to the center mansard-roofed portion of the hotel and would have resolved in the resort's other wing. What was left, however, was an unartful seam. Extensive work would be required to reimagine this exterior and also fill interior spaces with natural light. The elevation would also be significantly augmented via the carriage house wing. While slightly behind the main house, prominent carriage house doors would be in full view from this vantage point. Once renovated, the southern-faced façade would tell a far more proud story than the original.

FOLLOWING PAGES: A view of existing conditions at the front of the property prior to any renovation work.

LOOKING TO THE BAY

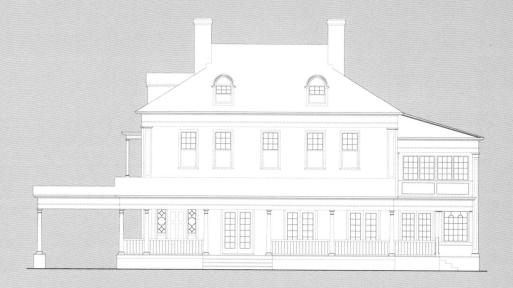

With a porch truncated abruptly into a screened porch area and a main entrance placed oddly to the side, the view of the house from the bay was uniquely frustrating. To reinsert a sense of logic and grandeur, I would augment and balance the residence architecturally, introducing the symmetry placed at the front on the rear elevation with abundant windows bringing long views of the bay into every room. Quietly stepped down from the main residence and the carriage house, a cabana space would exist anew, and areas for outdoor living would be generously developed.

FACING NORTH

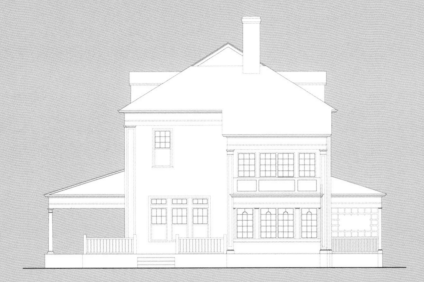

On the north side, two stories of sunrooms that appear to have been an enclosed addition made the roof feel askew, and stairs to what could have been a welcoming porch didn't resolve at doors into the home. As a result of this architectural confusion, I would completely reconsider the façade. Elements added on other sides would be reassuringly repeated, down to operable doors and dormers on the carriage house, windows with timeless green shutters, and an arched window at the roof's ridge line. The exterior change would be dramatic, though the historic narrative would persist.

FOLLOWING PAGES: The bay- and north-facing sides of the structure prior to renovation.

BELOW GRADE

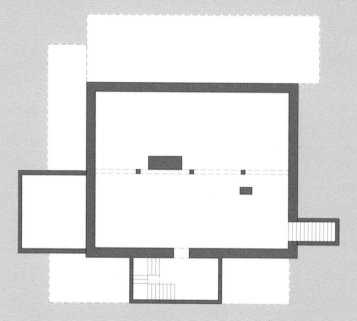

Underground, the existing basement was not much to speak of. With a stone foundation that naturally wept with condensation and a dirt floor, the space was unfinished and unusable. I would propose modifying the basement to provide extra square footage for a growing third generation of family that would begin to visit the property while adding finished dry storage space and a proper wine cellar for the homeowners' collection.

OPPOSITE: A view of the original stone foundation beneath the Myles Standish Hotel.

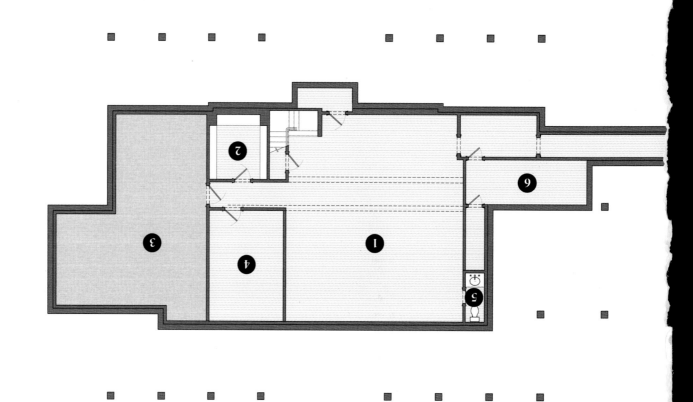

FLOOR PLAN LEGEND

- **1** Playroom
- **2** Wine Room
- **3** Mechanical Room
- **4** Craft Room
- **5** Powder Room
- **6** Storage Room No. 1
- **7** Storage Room No. 2

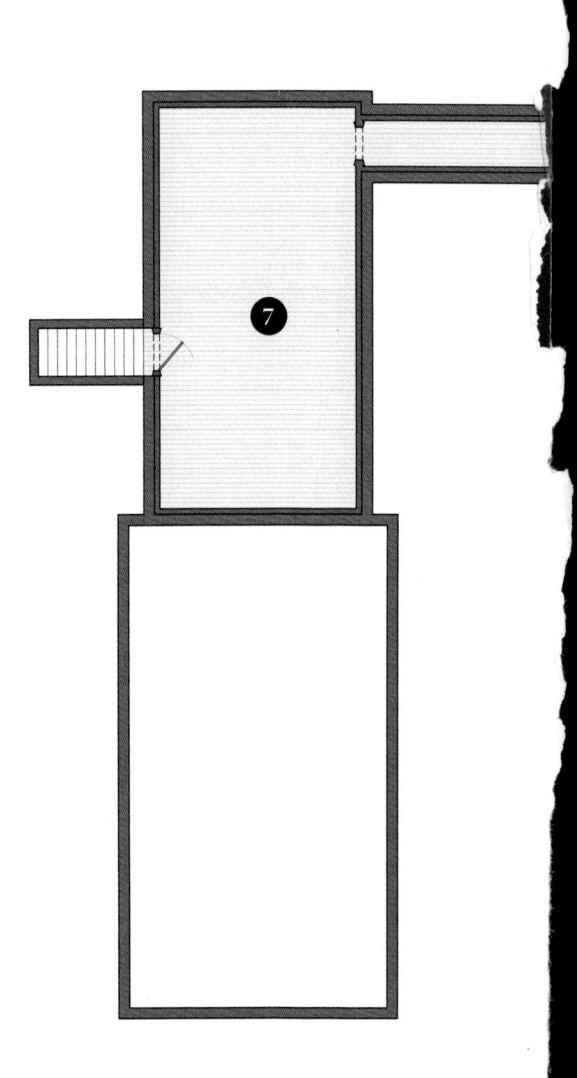

THE FIRST FLOOR

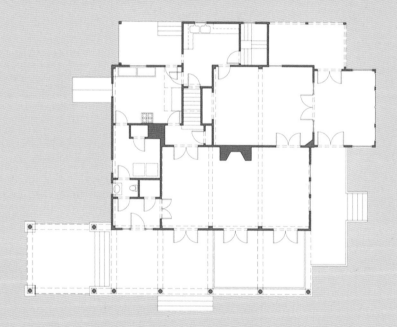

Only after careful study could the maze of rooms in the original structure be understood. Two working kitchens and a laundry greeted anyone who dared enter through the street-side arched trellis. Those who knew to drive around back for the main entrance entered a cramped foyer that seemed to be more of a vestibule. Just beyond, views from the living room were obstructed by a screened porch, and a sunroom and porch off the dining room seemed little-trafficked. The reimagined floor plan would completely transform the interior for today's modern family and would bear little resemblance to the original.

OPPOSITE: A view of the formal living room prior to construction.

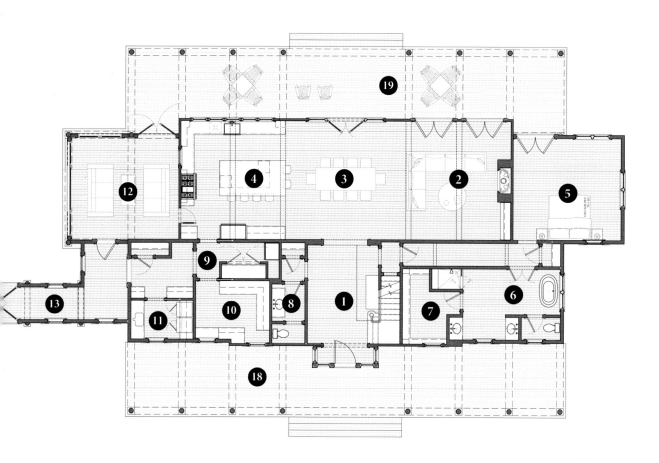

FLOOR PLAN LEGEND

1. Entry Foyer
2. Living Room
3. Dining Room
4. Kitchen
5. Primary Bedroom
6. Primary Bathroom
7. Primary Dressing Room
8. Powder Room
9. Pantry
10. Office & Storage
11. Laundry Room
12. Screened Porch
13. Gallery
14. Cabana
15. Cabana Bath
16. Side Entry
17. Carriage House Wing
18. Front Covered Porch
19. Rear Covered Porch

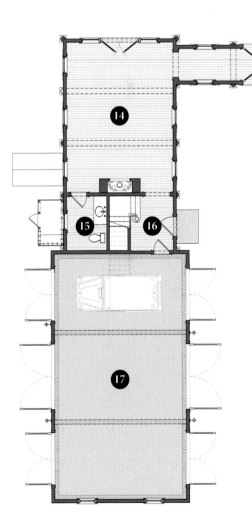

THE SECOND FLOOR

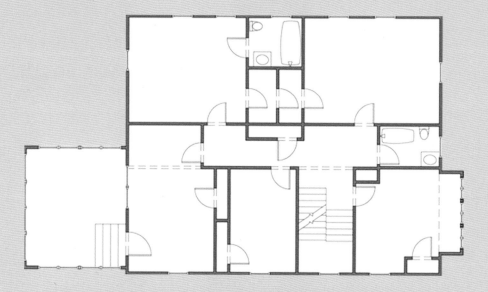

The original second-floor plan is representative of what might have existed in colonial homes of the early 1900s. The floor offered five bedrooms with the primary bedroom the only en-suite. A lone hall bath serviced the other four bedrooms. Reach-in closets were small by today's standards, and the central hall received natural light from a single stair window. In the proposed renovation, the second floor would become a bright modern family retreat with all en-suite bedrooms for privacy and balconies for indoor-outdoor luxury.

OPPOSITE: A view of the second floor enclosed sunroom prior to renovation.

THE THIRD FLOOR

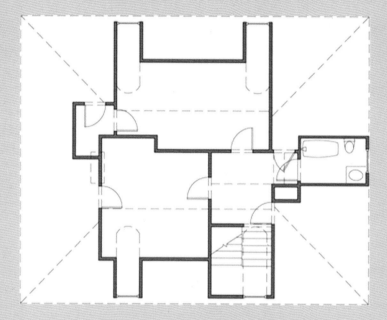

Two tight bedrooms and a bathroom were originally built under the eaves atop the third floor stair. While individual dormers brought some light into the space, the bedrooms felt cramped. My immediate want was to transform the third floor into true living space. I proposed opening the third floor completely, and adding a Nantucket dormer on the rear so that sunrises over the bay could be enjoyed from this high vantage point. With this approach, the third floor would be transformed into a magnificent office where homeowners could work while in residence.

OPPOSITE: An under-eave third floor bedroom prior to renovation.

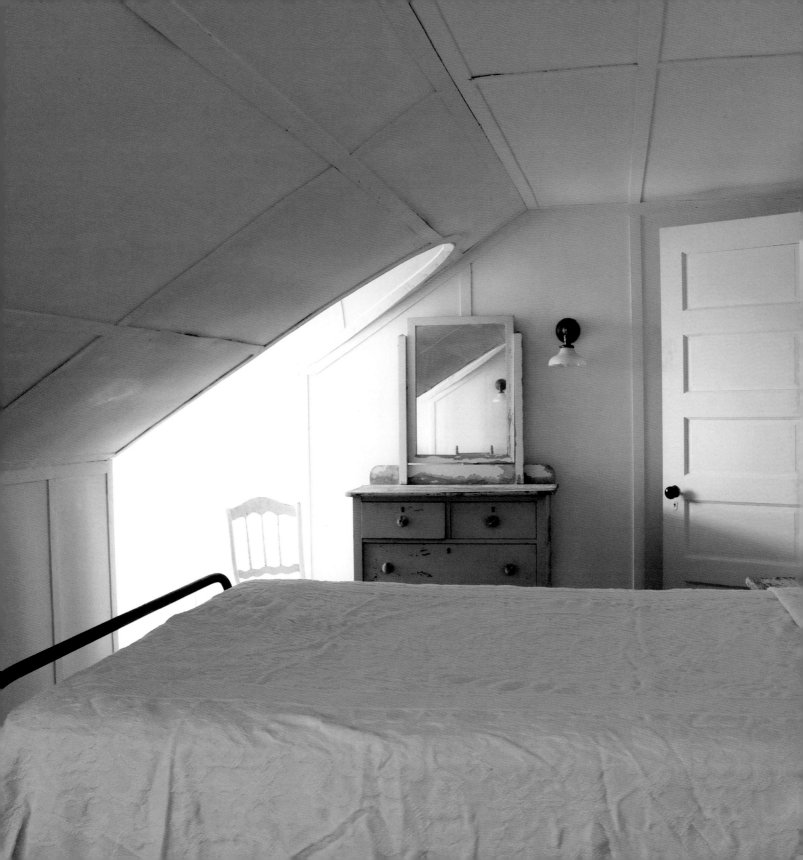

Chapter 2

BUILDING TOWARD THE FUTURE

W hen it comes to construction, the relationship between architect and builder is of paramount importance. In the best cases, a deep appreciation for each other's perspectives and trades exists, which requires a comprehensive understanding of each other's processes. Over the years, I've been fortunate to develop an exceptionally strong rapport with some of my most trusted partners, and as a result, when it came time

OPPOSITE: The front of the house is shown here just before renovation work began. Modifying this façade and the procession to it from the street would have tremendous impact on the property.

ABOVE: With the hotel wing lifted, the original foundation's composition of stone and brick is on display. To the side, the structure sits patiently atop steel beams, waiting for a new concrete foundation to be poured.

to tackle this project, I knew precisely who to recommend.

For the work at the Myles Standish, I called upon Steve Colclough and the masterful team at Colclough Construction. In more than 15 years of partnership and as many completed homes, I've come to rely on Steve and his crews for custom builds and restorations of the utmost quality. Their sensitivity to historical precedent and the craftsmanship of their staff and that of their subcontractors is exemplary.

Prior to beginning, we assessed existing conditions at the site. Every project has its own set of challenges, and the Myles Standish was no different. The most unique, however, related to an element which the clients and I agreed was an incredible asset—a towering *Kalopanax septemlobus* tree, which was centrally located in the front yard.

Commonly known as a castor aralia but rather uncommon overall, the tree produces clusters of white flowers in late summer and is regarded by the Arnold Arboretum of Harvard University as one of the best ornamental trees for the New England region. The existence of this tree on site was about as rare as the structure we were working on itself. While others may have considered removing it based on its placement, we took every possible step to protect the tree during construction and to incorporate it as an anchoring element of the home's new arrival sequence.

With substantial fencing encircling the tree to protect its trunk, branches, and formidable root system, construction could finally begin in

earnest. An old foundation of fieldstone and brick existed underneath the structure, with an uncanny patch of brick on the left side of the property. The bricked-off area was likely originally used for the hotel's ice or coal storage, and we could almost envision carriages being brought underneath the old structure to drop off the materials.

While rich with character, the old foundation would be insufficient to support the proposed renovations and additions, and a modern concrete foundation was specified. In order to pour it, however, the house needed to be methodically lifted and moved aside, then returned to the new foundation.

When it comes to renovating historic homes, lifting and moving a structure is often part of the program, and the process never fails to excite. First, holes need to be punched in the existing foundation. Those holes eventually receive steel beams which run through the entirety of the structure. In the case of the Myles Standish, the steel would support 75 tons of weight, which was comprised of framing, exterior shingles, windows, doors, and roofing. Once the track was set and casters were placed, a small excavator pulled the weight of the house to make room for the work to

Scan the code to see video of the house moving onto its new foundation.

PATRICK AHEARN

be done on the foundation.

Once the new concrete foundation was poured and backfilled, it was notched so the steel beams could be removed when the house was set back down. A track was then readied to slide the house over. Once pushed, it was subsequently lowered and secured. All of the old subfloor was then removed and all of the floor joists were reset.

The challenge with buildings of the Myles Standish's vintage is that structurally, over time, exterior walls can begin to bow. At this particular project, the walls were incredibly bowed, which had to be addressed in advance of any interior work. To rectify the problem, the house needed to be released from everything that was pressing its walls outward. The centerline of the roof was cut free, and the crows foot and every rafter tail were cut as well. Then the roof was slowly and carefully raised a quarter inch at a time. In total, the roof was raised more than three inches to allow the structure to be leveled and plumbed. Every single wall and the entire roof system—every bit of it was completely redone to ensure the property would be structurally sound for the future.

With the house supported firmly on its concrete foundation and now newly leveled and plumbed, additional work could begin. A few items from the original hotel had already been removed, including decorative doors from built-in cabinetry in the dining room, a clock from the hotel's old mantel, and a granite step which would have been placed so guests could easily exit a stagecoach at the hotel's front door. The cabinet doors would be given new life in a pantry, the

clock would be fully restored and displayed in the foyer, and the step would stay near the front porch as a nod to the past.

Architecturally, however, one of the most significant elements to be saved was a dormer on the side elevation of the residence, and removing it proved no small feat. The entire piece had to be surgically cut from the roofline and craned to the ground. Once there, a skilled team rebuilt the dormer while the overall house was being secured. After the roof was lifted, the dormer was hoisted back into place. A rolled copper roof was then installed, designed expressly to tie into the chimney and a new window, protecting a complicated connection from the elements.

The chimneys themselves represented a surprise. In any build, unforeseen needs are inevitable, and at the Myles Standish, the original chimneys were an unfortunate problem. Once the project was underway, it became clear that the chimneys were structurally unsound and could not be salvaged. With great care, they were taken down and rebuilt to the exact specifications and dimensions of the originals. Our goal in replicating and reconstructing them was to preserve the legitimacy of the architecture and the integrity of the home.

As with many projects, a few pivots were made on site as construction proceeded. A third floor bathroom tucked inside a dormer was eliminated, and a separate space above the carriage house wing was configured for an in-house fitness center. These modifications represent a positive partnership between builder, architect, and client

PREVIOUS PAGES: With the new concrete foundation poured and set, the original structure is moved into place. Framing for the carriage house is simultaneously underway.

ABOVE: A new story for the Myles Standish begins. The original structure has been moved onto a new foundation which can support its weight and that of additions, while the connector links the residence to the stepped-down carriage house wing.

PATRICK AHEARN

and were key to the home's successful and smooth completion.

Overall, the build represented a true marriage of old and new. In the completed home, there may be some old joists, framing, and sheathing, but any additional parts that were constructed or patched in were painstakingly matched to the originals. The other item of note is that the entire home is made of wood. Top to bottom, the only plaster on site is within closets and in an unfinished area of the basement. Walls are clad in beadboard as would have been done in seaside New England homes of yesteryear, and significant millwork was specified including cased openings and crown molding to indicate both quality and history.

In more than eight months of construction, skilled laborers and craftsmen all lent their time and proficiency to the home. Master carpenters, cabinetmakers, tilers, landscapers, and so many more—all played a part in creating this historically inspired composition. Thanks to their dedication the home feels authentic inside and out.

It takes a talented team to renovate a much older home with today's modern materials. The process is far more complicated than new construction and represents a property's renaissance, a rebirth that can allow a residence to live for centuries more. The work-in-progress photos on the pages in this chapter are a testament to the hardworking crewmembers who had a hand in this build, without whom the property's next phase would not be possible.

PREVIOUS PAGES: A continuous porch is framed along the rear of the house, its canopy ready to accept cedar roof shingles which already appear atop the carriage house, cabana, and connector. Original third floor dormers have not yet been removed.

OPPOSITE: The formidable castor aralia is seen in the foreground of this construction photo surrounded by protective fencing while the home's exterior is prepared for siding.

PATRICK AHEARN

Chapter 3

NEW LIFE FOR THE MYLES STANDISH HOTEL

The finished residence is a testament to narrative-driven architecture and proves that aging structures can indeed be revived for uncompromised modern living. Expanded for its next phase, the reinterpretation emulates the sentiment of the original hotel while manifesting a contemporary approach to life within. The home clearly communicates its history while living proudly for the future as a seaside estate in timeless tradition.

OPPOSITE: A view from above showcases how the reimagination takes full advantage of the site while preserving the historic significance of the property.

The Front Exterior

A dramatic transformation is noted from the street, where you can all but hear the clack of horse hooves proceed around the castor aralia while teams tinker with watercrafts as saltwater breezes waft through the boathouse. Elements of grandeur have been added—including proud columns supporting the front porch canopy on the main house, the gallery connector wing, and the overall carriage house program—all while keeping within the spirit of the originally conceived resort. What began as an obscure hotel wing has been reconceived with clear architectural thought, even as it has been augmented with substantial new programming.

OPPOSITE: While the structure has been augmented and reinterpreted for present day, elements of history remain including a sizeable stone wall which became part of the overall arrival sequence.

PATRICK AHEARN

PREVIOUS PAGES: A more than 100-year-old castor aralia tree is as much a feature on the property as the architecture itself.

ABOVE: The reimagined property makes thoughtful use of nooks and crannies on site. The outdoor shower shown at left is thoughtfully nestled into a hidden corner for privacy.

RIGHT: The carriage house appears to have been a boat shed connected to the main residence over time. Functional doors on the front and back of the building can be opened to allow bay breezes to pass through the structure.

NEW LIFE FOR THE MYLES STANDISH HOTEL

OPPOSITE: A fall sunset bathes the home's proud brick chimneys and white clapboard siding in a warm glow.

RIGHT: Historically inspired details like the copper coach lights seen beside the main entrance add to the residence's narrative. A plaque from the Duxbury Rural and Historical Society is proudly featured at the front of the structure.

FOLLOWING PAGES: Two sets of French doors in the gallery connecting the carriage house to the main house act as a separate entrance from the motor court to the rear terrace and outdoor entertainment area.

NORTH WING OF THE
STANDISH HOUSE
1872
D.R.H.S.

THE REAR EXTERIOR & AREAS FOR OUTDOOR LIVING

A newly prioritized indoor-outdoor program is at once apparent in the reimagined rear exterior. Drawn to the outside by expansive views, visitors find themselves on a covered porch with painted columns and architectural finishes that reinforce the space as an extension of the interior. Victorian lawn games may have given way to bluestone terraces and an inviting pool, but the detailing on the exterior harkens back to another time, supporting the home's historic narrative. The placement of the aquatic program along the side of the property balances the carriage house wing on the opposite of the connector gallery while preserving the expansive rear lawn for entertaining.

OPPOSITE: Purposeful indoor-outdoor connection was inserted throughout the rear of the property along with an aquatic program and significant hardscape.

PATRICK AHEARN

LEFT: On the rear portion of the main house, I revived the porch as it was originally intended, as an unobstructed place to enjoy the magnificence of the bay along the entirety of the structure. Affectionately referred to as "the hippo highway," the line in the grass was created by the homeowners' Scottish terriers Wallace and Annie, whose bodies have carved a natural pathway in the grass much the way hippos' bodies do through the African savanna.

PATRICK AHEARN

ABOVE: Previously truncated on one side due to the former screened porch, the new covered porch can now be accessed from either side and the rear yard thanks to modified design and placement.

RIGHT: A veritable outdoor oasis now exists at the rear of the property. From the covered porch to the screened porch and exterior grill station, dining area, pool, and fireplace, every opportunity was maximized to promote the site's natural magnificence. Wallace, one of the homeowners' Scottish terriers, enjoys his perch on the new stone retaining wall.

PREVIOUS PAGES: From cedar roof shingles, white siding, and Essex green shutters with traditional holdbacks to copper coach lights dotting the composition, the renovated structure is a study in timeless architecture.

OPPOSITE: Consideration was given toward creating spaces for outdoor living that could be used year-round, including this new outdoor fireplace.

RIGHT: Panoramic views across the lawn were purposefully preserved in order to fully appreciate the site from the new rear terrace.

LEFT: Instead of taking over the center of the landscape, the bayfront pool was carefully placed to the side, allowing for sweeping views across the rear yard.

FOLLOWING TWO SPREADS: The hierarchy of structures on site is clearly delineated no matter the view. The main house takes the lead, with the carriage house beside it stepped down in scale, and the deftly attached gallery and pool cabana stepped down even further.

PATRICK AHEARN

LIFE ON THE FIRST FLOOR

Within the first floor, history meets present day in a distinguished residence of exceptional quality. A spine anchored at the front door entices visitors with views of the bay and encourages movement through the space. Ceiling heights are just over 10½ feet, achieving open, inviting volume that feels human-scale instead of cavernous. Large windows and French doors illuminate the space and offer captivating water views at every turn.

Experiencing the new seamless flow from the kitchen to the dining and living areas, it's hard to conceive the maze of closed-off rooms that previously existed within the property.

OPPOSITE: The gallery connecting the main residence to the cabana and carriage house allows for everyday enjoyment of artwork. Architectural details including a coffered ceiling and beams, beadboard, and shutters elevate the space to more than a mere passageway.

PATRICK AHEARN

OPPOSITE: The structure we were originally presented lacked a foyer. Our renovation added a welcoming open foyer befitting a seaside estate property complete with a bright vestibule and architecturally detailed walls and ceiling.

RIGHT: Now logically resolving in the front foyer, a grand formal stair leads all the way to the top of the home. Custom millwork throughout elevates the space.

PATRICK AHEARN

OPPOSITE: From the foyer, one looks through the dining room out to the bay beyond the French doors. This central spine was inserted into the home's architecture purposefully, encouraging flow through the home and capitalizing on water views.

RIGHT: The casual family room was made for modern living, and enjoys views of the bay from a comfortable space in which the family can relax. French doors open to the covered rear porch, connecting the interior with the outdoor program.

LEFT AND OPPOSITE: The property was fully outfitted for today's family with an open concept kitchen featuring a wall of glass to capitalize on unobstructed views out to the water. It is hard to believe that two cumbrous cooking spaces previously existed within the property; this very significant architectural change—an open concept kitchen with oversized island—represents a meaningful modernization of the residence.

LEFT: The pantry features a subtle nod to the past. Featured in the hotel's dining room built-ins, the unique glass-front cabinet doors were preserved and incorporated as part of new cabinetry.

OPPOSITE: A first floor laundry serves as a utilitarian space with expanded function housing pool towels for guests and grandchildren.

RIGHT: The concept of the screened porch, albeit not its precise placement, was preserved and incorporated into the new design, allowing for outdoor enjoyment beyond summer months.

NEW LIFE FOR THE MYLES STANDISH HOTEL

OPPOSITE: In the connector gallery, two pairs of opposing French doors can be simultaneously opened to create a direct pathway from the front of the house to aquatic programming and exterior entertaining areas at the rear.

RIGHT: The connector expertly links the main residence to the pool cabana shown here and the carriage house just beyond. A set of French doors opens this lounge to the pool terrace outside.

LEFT: More casual finishes are noted inside the carriage house down to the squared balusters supporting the handrail on the stair up to the family fitness center.

OPPOSITE: Horizontal shiplap on the walls and stained shiplap and beams on the ceiling all indicate a more relaxed vibe inside the cabana space.

Dramatic moments are established within the new first-floor primary bedroom suite. (OPPOSITE) A new vaulted ceiling allows for oversized modern fixtures within classically detailed walls. (RIGHT) Serenity and privacy are preserved inside the primary bathroom, with a wall of windows featuring operable interior shutters.

Private Spaces on the Second & Third Floors

An elevated level of millwork carries upstairs, decorating walls of the stairway that begin in the formal foyer and those of adjoining hallways. Rooms that open to these halls—including second floor bedroom chambers and the third floor library—feature somewhat more casual and coastally relevant beadboard juxtaposed with more formal moldings to create an atmosphere that feels at once comfortable and refined. This presentation of architectural trim reinforces the narrative of the home as a magnificent resort of yesteryear while keeping with how people want to live today.

OPPOSITE: Anchored in the foyer, three floors of stairway climb from the main level to the third floor of the home. Exceptional millwork is seen throughout, including architectural wall paneling, beadboard, and cased built-ins.

Architectural wall paneling including beadboard and shiplap carries through private spaces on the second floor, and historically inspired hardware including doorknobs and hinges were specified throughout. (OPPOSITE) The homeowner's grandfather's framed bathing costume from the 1920s makes for a personal touch that's perfectly on theme. (RIGHT) Bay views are appreciated from three out of four upstairs bedrooms.

LEFT: An expansive second floor bathroom includes its own balcony from which guests can enjoy the saltwater air and serene bay views.

PATRICK AHEARN

In the light-filled third floor open office and library, full expressed rooflines and classic details abound. (LEFT) The interior of an original preserved dormer is now dressed with beadboard and traditional casings. (OPPOSITE) A period-appropriate arched window was inserted to allow natural light to illuminate the space on all sides.

In the Snow

We often assume waterfront properties to be summer retreats, but the hotel-turned-residence is lived in and appreciated year-round. Against a backdrop of winter, the historic narrative is clearly defined, with the main residence leading the storyline and offering deferential attention to the past. Covered in white, the white clapboard of the Myles Standish all but rises from the earth beneath it, and appears as though it has stood forever.

OPPOSITE: White snow all but reflects off the colonnade supporting the front porch's canopy at the renovated Myles Standish Hotel.

PATRICK AHEARN

PREVIOUS PAGES: Mother nature's blanket
of white covers the front lawn. With the
formidable tree dormant, the architecture of
the front of the house is more clearly in view.

OPPOSITE: A quiet, chilly view of the rear of
the property in winter.

FOLLOWING PAGES: Thanks to a complete
modernization of all systems and the most
advanced insulation materials, the energy-
efficient renovated property is appreciated
year-round.

Chapter 4

PAST MEETS PRESENT

In a project with history as significant as the Myles Standish, we often uncover remnants from the past during construction. Whether found beneath floorboards or buried in the earth, these relics are reminders of life on the property before present times. We are pleased to share some of the findings in these pages, along with some very special hotel artifacts and ephemera that are now part of the homeowners' personal collection.

_____

OPPOSITE: This is no ordinary sea glass. Pieces of glass bottles from Standish Spring beverages wash up on bay beaches to this day.

While there weren't any diaries found in wall cavities or old photos in the attic at this property, there was an abundance of glass that appeared as we excavated which related directly to the hotel's history.

Toward the bayfront, a natural spring exists on the property. Local folklore has it that early settlers drank this water, and today the spring still trickles, attracting all sorts of wildlife to sip from its stream.

Enterprising hotel proprietors L. Boyer and Sons bottled the spring water in the late 1800s and sold it nationwide according to the Duxbury Rural and Historical Society. Capitalizing on the Myles Standish name, they eventually sold beverages including lemon soda and ginger ale in addition to natural spring water. The glass found in the land as we dug is believed to be from the bottling company, as surely the rare intact vessels would indicate. New Myles Standish Hotel homeowners find pieces of glass from these bottles on shore with frequency and keep them as a reminder of the past, and a collection of Standish Spring bottles and remnants is now enjoyed as outdoor decor in hurricane vessels at the residence.

Beyond the bottles, other items from the hotel's glory days have been passed from owner to owner. Pieces from the hotel's original silver place settings have been preserved, all engraved with the hotel name. A cannonball from a cannon formerly on site and door knockers from each bedroom have been saved along with a granite step used for assistance when exiting stagecoaches upon arrival at the property. A clock which at one point featured prominently on the hotel mantel has been completely refurbished and newly preserved. Metal-lined wooden crates may have acted as early cold boxes for milk deliveries, or possibly for the Standish Springs bottles themselves, and a vintage bedroom scale now has a place in the home fitness center.

Chimes that would have been played more than a century ago are a perennial favorite from the old hotel. While we can't know precisely what they indicated, to hear them ring strikes a nostalgic chord of wonder, much like the one cued when experiencing the reinterpreted property itself.

OPPOSITE: A rare intact bottle from the Standish Spring dates to the early 1900s or possibly just prior. The natural spring still runs on-site.

PATRICK AHEARN

OPPOSITE AND RIGHT: Prior owners had mounted a clock that was original to the hotel on the wall in their main entry, though it may have featured prominently on a hotel mantel decades prior. My clients had the clock completely refurbished, and an architecturally detailed built-in was designed to prominently feature it in the renovated foyer.

FOLLOWING PAGES: A series of silver spoons produced by Reed & Barton engraved with Myles Standish Hotel nomenclature. At the turn of the century, fine resorts typically presented actual silver during meal service.

LEFT: A wooden box with hammered metal interior compartments may have been used for milk delivery or early refrigeration.

OPPOSITE: A framed bathing costume from the 1920s is part of the homeowners' personal collection. Purchased on nearby Nantucket, it adds to the home's overall thematic presentation and implied history.

OPPOSITE AND RIGHT: At the
time of purchase in 2016, each
bedroom held its own scale.
Whether the scales were placed
in the rooms from the time of
the hotel's inception is unknown;
current homeowners have kept
one working scale in their fitness
center.

PATRICK AHEARN

Scan the code to hear the chimes ring.

RIGHT: One of the most charming elements to survive from the Myles Standish Hotel is this set of musical chimes. Perhaps sounded to indicate the start of a meal or an activity, the chimes are still delightfully functional today.

PAST MEETS PRESENT

ACKNOWLEDGMENTS

As a case study in historic renovation and reimagination, the Myles Standish Hotel project has given me the opportunity to share my processes from start to finish with architecture enthusiasts, students, clients, and friends. As an architect, I revel in learning the history of a place and bringing it forward in the way people want to live today while being sensitive to context and the space and scale of a community. This book has encapsulated that joy of process, learning, and completion.

None of this book would have been possible without the incredible care and consideration that homeowners Steve and Alicia Bolze put into the property. A project like this one takes vision and willingness to take a leap of faith, and they jumped in wholeheartedly from day one. With the Bolzes shepherding the structure into the future, a historic half-hotel was preserved and revived instead of being demolished, and I share their pride in that renewal. As we worked, Steve and Alicia fell in love with the house and chose to move from their residence next door into this beautiful new home. Their enthusiasm for our work and commitment to the property is nothing short of tremendous. I wish them many years of enjoyment and memories on Duxbury Bay—their partnership on this project was a gift.

I would be remiss if I didn't also acknowledge the talented teams at Colclough Construction and a Blade of Grass. I rely on Steve and Matt Colclough and their crews for a quality finished product time and again—we've done so for more than a decade, and I look forward to decades more. For landscape design and construction at the Myles Standish Hotel, a Blade of Grass developed a natural backdrop complementary to our architecture and a program befitting this elevated seaside estate. To work with teams of each of their caliber is a pleasure.

Thanks to the team at my own office, we're able to bring projects like the Myles Standish Hotel to life year after year. I like to say we see with the same set of eyes and collectively believe in the same approach to creating timeless architecture. With the positive response to our work, we have grown, and I am particularly grateful for Michael Tartamella, AIA, whose day-to-day leadership of the firm is invaluable, and for the core team that has been with me for many years.

In addition, I applaud the Duxbury Historical Commission's ongoing work to protect the authenticity and historic integrity of their town. My architecture is rooted in the notion that historical context creates the foundation of timeless design, and without commissions like theirs, too often proud structures from the past are demolished. I would also like to acknowledge past president and founding member of the Duxbury Historical Commission Peter Talbot Smith, AIA, RIBA, whose ties to the town run deep and whose efforts to preserve the local vernacular are laudable. Thanks also to Pamela Campbell, AIA, who has helmed the Duxbury Historical Commission and carries the torch for new building designs compatible with the town's existing architecture. I am thankful to each of them for their enthusiasm for this project, their passion for Duxbury history, and their willingness to be involved.

Separately, the direct involvement of the Duxbury Rural and Historical Society in this book has allowed me to share actual visuals from the past with readers. Thanks to archivist and historian Carolyn Ravenscroft, many historical photos, advertisements, and ephemera are included, enriching these pages and rounding out the story. My appreciation also goes to Duxbury town historian Tony Kelso, whose oral history and knowledge provided a clear understanding of what actually happened to the center portion of the hotel.

In addition, I appreciate the contributions of the Historic Preservation Office of the Mashpee Wampanoag Tribe, and thank Tribal Councilman David Weeden for his direction regarding proper nomenclature and historical accuracy.

So many had a hand in producing this volume. I would like to thank ORO Editions for their ongoing support for my work, especially managing editor Jake Anderson who it's great to work with once again. Thank you to my writer Caroline Stone, whose way with words benefitted

this narrative and continues to impact our firm every day. And to Katherine Nolan, whose expertise as director of marketing has been critical not only to the development of this book but to its ongoing promotion, and whose thoughtful design showcases the evolution of the project so effectively.

In addition, I offer my gratitude and thanks to Taylor Ahearn, whose photography has wonderfully captured the essence of our architecture and sense of place that was reestablished at the Myles Standish Hotel. I'm glad to call her my photographer and am even more proud to call her my daughter.

The idea for this book originated when the Myles Standish Hotel project won a 2021 Bulfinch Award. Granted annually by the New England chapter of the Institute of Classical Architecture and Art, the awards recognize professionals across the nation who are committed to promoting excellence in the classical tradition and allied arts. Thank you to the ICAA for recognizing this project, and for sparking the idea that it should be shared.

PROJECT AND
BOOK CREDITS

BUILDER Colclough Construction
KITCHEN DESIGN Christopher Peacock
INTERIOR DESIGNER Homeowners
LANDSCAPE A Blade of Grass

TEXT BY Patrick Ahearn
WRITTEN WITH Caroline Stone
P.A. ARCHITECT MARKETING DIRECTOR Katherine Nolan
MARKETING Caroline Stone
ORO EDITIONS MANAGING DIRECTOR Jake Anderson
BOOK DESIGNER Katherine Nolan

PREVIOUS PAGES: With the renovation of the Myles Standish Hotel complete, the structure can once again host events as it did in its heyday. Shown on prior pages is the first celebration held by the owners marking their son's engagement.

PHOTOGRAPHY CREDITS

Taylor Ahearn: jacket, pages 6, 8–9, 28, 88, 90–98, 100–114, 116–132, 134–139, 148, 150, 152–161, 168
Randi Baird Photography: jacket headshot
Cara Szczebak: pages 164–165
Colclough Construction: pages 48–49, 74, 76, 78–79, 81–84
Duxbury Rural & Historical Society: pages 10, 12, 14–17, 25–26
Hawk Visuals: pages 2–3, 86
Homeowners: pages 18–19, 32–33, 38–39
Ian Dagnall / Alamy Stock Photo: page 21
Ingrid Nappellio: pages 30–31, 37, 56–57, 61, 65, 69, 73
Tony & Jane Kelso: page 34
Mauritius Images GmbH / Alamy Stock Photo: page 22
Neil Landino: pages 140, 142–143, 145–147
Patrick Ahearn Architect: end sheets, pages 41–47, 50–55, 58–60, 62–64, 66–68, 70–72

FOLLOWING PAGE: Annie watches over the front motor court through a low windowpane in a front-facing French door.